BUG LIFE CYCLES

By Rod Barkman

GRASSHOPPER

KidHaven PUBLISHING

Published in 2027 by
KidHaven Publishing, an Imprint of Greenhaven Publishing, LLC
2544 Clinton St., Buffalo, NY 14224

Written by: Rod Barkman
Edited by: Noah Leatherland
Designed by: Amelia Harris

All facts, statistics, web addresses, and URLs in this book were verified as valid and accurate at time of writing. No responsibility for any changes to external websites or references can be accepted by either the author or publisher.

Cataloging-in-Publication Data

Names: Barkman, Rod.
Title: Grasshopper / Rod Barkman.
Description: Buffalo, NY : KidHaven Publishing, 2027. | Series: Bug life cycles | Includes glossary and index.
Identifiers: ISBN 9781534571037 (pbk.) | ISBN 9781534571044 (library bound) | ISBN 9781534571051 (ebook)
Subjects: LCSH: Grasshoppers--Juvenile literature. | Grasshoppers--Life cycles--Juvenile literature.
Classification: LCC QL508.A2 B37 2027 | DDC 595.726--dc23

Printed in China

CPSIA compliance information: Batch #QS27KH: For further information contact Greenhaven Publishing LLC at 1-844-317-7404.

PHOTO CREDITS

All images are courtesy of Shutterstock.com, unless otherwise stated.

Cover – ShaziaPhotoGhrapher, Alexander Denisenko, Anastasiia Hevko. 2–3 – Glass and Nature. 4–5 – ViewStock, Unique Marketing, Q88, Inside Creative House, Bangkok Click Studio, 1st footage. 6–7 – Jack Wada, Insan1919. 8–9 – goran_safarek, CHA ATCHARA. 10–11 – Rizky Ade Jonathan, bepsy. 12–13 – Karla Guerrero Carrillo, Halomarlo. 14–15 – Rani Erni, Protasov AN. 16–17 – Antonphotograp, lessysebastian. 18–19 – Peter Milota Jr, Bhoopendra_kumar54, Eleanor Esterhuizen, Matyas Rehak. 20–21 – I Wayan Sumatika, Elina Litovkina. 22–23 – Director_Nara2424, Russell Marshall, studiojassmerah, Eileen Kumpf.

CONTENTS

Words that look like this can be found in the glossary on page 24.

WHAT ARE LIFE CYCLES?

Every living thing has a life cycle. Life cycles are the stages of growth and change that a living thing goes through. These changes include the start of life, growth, reproduction, and death.

The life of a human begins as a baby. The baby grows into a toddler, then a child, and then a teenager. When the human being grows into an adult, they may make babies of their own before growing old.

MEET THE GRASSHOPPER

Grasshoppers are jumping insects with powerful legs. Their bodies are made up of three main parts—the head, thorax, and abdomen. Grasshoppers have antennae on their heads that help them feel the world around them.

Grasshoppers can be found on every continent, except Antarctica. They are usually brown and green in color. This helps them blend in with their surroundings.

Can you spot the grasshopper?

EGG

The first stage in a grasshopper's life cycle is the egg. Female grasshoppers lay fertilized eggs under sand or fallen leaves. They then spray a sticky, foamy liquid on the eggs. This liquid hardens and protects the eggs.

THIS FEMALE GRASSHOPPER IS LAYING HER EGGS IN SAND.

Females lay their eggs in pods, which are clumps of eggs. Grasshopper eggs are small. There can be anywhere between 10 and 300 eggs in a pod, depending on the species of grasshopper.

NYMPH

Grasshopper eggs hatch in the spring. The baby is called a nymph. Usually, all the nymphs from a pod hatch within a few minutes of each other. The nymph's body has a hard outer skin called an exoskeleton to protect it.

Nymphs must shed their skin as they get bigger over time. This is because their exoskeletons do not grow or change. Grasshopper nymphs shed their skin four to six times as they grow into adults.

Grasshopper nymphs do not have working wings yet.

ADULT GRASSHOPPER

For most species of grasshoppers, nymphs become adults once they have grown their wings. This happens after five to six weeks. Adult grasshoppers can reach over 4 inches (10 cm) long, depending on the species.

Some species of grasshoppers never grow wings.

Once a nymph becomes an adult grasshopper, the adult lives for around two to three months. Altogether, many grasshoppers have a lifespan of about 12 months. Adult grasshoppers usually live in open areas such as grasslands.

HOW GRASSHOPPERS LIVE

Most grasshoppers are herbivores. This means that they only eat plants. Grasshoppers are able to eat several times their own body weight in a day.

Some types of grasshoppers go through a phase of swarming. This is when millions of grasshoppers migrate together. Grasshoppers that swarm like this are known as locusts.

Swarms of locusts eat huge amounts of plants, including food grown for humans.

Grasshoppers have powerful legs. Some can jump up to 3 feet (1 m) in distance. This leaping ability helps grasshoppers stay safe. If a predator comes close, they can quickly jump away.

Male grasshoppers can make a buzzing sound. This is known as singing. Grasshoppers make this sound by rubbing their ridged back legs against their wings. This sound is part of the grasshoppers' mating ritual.

TYPES OF GRASSHOPPERS

also known as the rainbow grasshopper

large, flightless grasshopper the size of a mouse

It is thought that there are over 10,000 species of grasshoppers in the world. Here are a few with interesting features.

bright colors warn predators that it is poisonous

vivid red and blue pattern on its back wings

END OF LIFE

Just like all living things, a grasshopper eventually reaches the end of its life. Grasshoppers are often eaten by predators such as birds, lizards, spiders, and rodents.

The life cycle of a grasshopper does not end, though. If the grasshopper has mated, the female will lay eggs. This gives life to more grasshoppers, and the life cycle continues.

LIFE CYCLE OF A GRASSHOPPER

A grasshopper changes over the stages of its life cycle until it is able to mate and make more grasshoppers.

A grasshopper's life begins as an egg buried in soil. The egg hatches, and a grasshopper nymph comes out. The nymph eats, sheds its skin, and grows until it becomes an adult and finds a mate.

GLOSSARY

fertilized to do with eggs that have been changed by material from the male of the species

hatch to break out of an egg

mated to have produced young with an animal of the same species

mating ritual behaviors that an animal uses to attract a mate

migrate when lots of animals move across a great distance

predator an animal that hunts other animals for food

reproduction making more of the same type of thing

species a group of very similar animals or plants that can make babies together

vivid bright and striking

INDEX